"Lara Honos-Webb's book contains forty activities for helping teenagers with ADHD thrive and excel at home, in social situations, and at school. *The ADHD Workbook for Teens* is an essential guide that will help teens with ADHD have successful lives."

—Stephanie Moulton Sarkis, Ph.D., NCC, LMHC, author of *10 Simple Solutions to Adult ADD*, *Making the Grade with ADD*, *ADD and Your Money*, and *Adult ADD*

"This thought-provoking workbook offers teens confidence, reassurance, motivation, and insight. Thank you, Lara Honos-Webb, for letting teenagers know that ADHD is a gift that is full of opportunities. It's a message teens with ADHD deserve."

—Robin Goldstein, Ph.D., faculty member at Johns Hopkins University and author of *The New Baby Answer Book.*

D0824847

the adhd workbook for teens

activities to help you
gain motivation
and **confidence**

LARA HONOS-WEBB, PH.D.

Instant Help Books
A Division of New Harbinger Publications, Inc.

Distributed in Canada by Raincoast Books

Copyright © 2010 by Lara Honos-Webb
        Instant Help Books
        A Division of New Harbinger Publications, Inc.
        5674 Shattuck Avenue
        Oakland, CA 94609
        www.newharbinger.com

Cover design by Amy Shoup

Library of Congress Cataloging-in-Publication Data

Honos-Webb, Lara.
  The ADHD workbook for teens / Lara Honos-Webb.
    p. cm.
  Includes bibliographical references and index.
  ISBN 978-1-57224-865-6 (pbk. : alk. paper) -- ISBN 978-1-57224-866-3 (pdf ebook : alk. paper) 1. Attention-deficit disorder in adolescence--Popular works. 2. Attention-deficit disorder in adolescence--Problems, exercises, etc. I. Title.
  RJ506.H9H656 2010
  616.85'8900835--dc22

                2010040282

14   13   12

10   9   8   7   6   5   4

I gratefully dedicate this book to Ken, Kenny, and Audrey Webb for giving me the gift of waking up happy every day.

contents

✳ contents

A Note from the Author

Dear Reader,

This book offers you a chance to make a major change in your life: to begin to define yourself by what you do well rather than by your weaknesses. For the rest of your life, you can benefit from focusing on what is working rather than what is not working.

Sometimes teens with ADHD think that they are not on the same playing field as others, but that is not true. ADHD does, however, present many challenges for teens, and this book will give you tools to deal with those challenges. For example, you will learn some basic resources for building your motivation and confidence, which can help you achieve the goals you set for yourself.

ADHD comes with gifts as well as challenges. You will learn to find your gifts and interests and use those to build your motivation and confidence. Many teens with ADHD are creative, emotionally sensitive, and good at reading others. While these very gifts may create challenges in getting good grades, they offer opportunities for success in many arenas and career choices.

You'll read success stories of teens who overcame the significant challenges of ADHD. You'll meet teens who increased their motivation by realizing that there were many careers that involved their most passionate interests and didn't require them to sit still all day. You'll meet teens who gained confidence as they discovered their many gifts they had literally not been paying attention to. You'll meet teens who built skills for staying organized and finding resources to solve specific problems of ADHD.

Although you may be tempted to skim through the book, I encourage you to slow down and actually complete the activities. You'll be amazed at how simple shifts in perspective can bring you lasting benefits. You can practice skills like challenging negative thoughts that pop up in your mind and deep breathing to calm yourself down. You will learn to take control of your thoughts and to feel emotions that can lead to healing. The harder you try, the more you can change your life.

for you to know

Having ADHD means that you are different from others in what you pay attention to. Your teachers and parents may complain that you have difficulty focusing on schoolwork or following directions. Others may complain you are too hyper. Your own reactions may vary as well; it's normal to have mixed feelings—both positive and negative—about the diagnosis of ADHD.

Robby was relieved when he found out that he had ADHD. It helped to explain why he struggled so much in school, but he was still afraid he would never measure up to others.

When Megan was diagnosed with ADHD, she thought it meant that she was not as smart as other kids.

Jacob actually hoped he had ADHD. He told his mom that all the cool and creative kids in his school had ADHD.

for you to do

Did you feel better about yourself before or after you got your diagnosis?

_____

_____

_____

What was the upside of getting the diagnosis?

_____

_____

_____

What was the downside of getting the diagnosis?

_____

_____

_____

How has your diagnosis helped you better understand yourself?

_____

_____

_____

... and more to do

Different people have different ideas about ADHD. Tell whether you agree or disagree with these two statements, and why.

Teens with ADHD are less intelligent than others.

_____

_____

_____

_____

Teens with ADHD are creative, unique, and gifted.

_____

_____

_____

_____

What are some other things you think or have heard about ADHD?

_____

_____

_____

_____

2 when is your ADHD a problem?

for you to know

Your ADHD symptoms may create problems at times, but in many situations they won't. For example, the more interested you are in a subject or activity, the more you will be able to focus and pay attention. If you can figure out when your symptoms are at their worst—like in a classroom or sitting through long lectures—you will know when you most need to work on dealing with them.

Scott got good grades in school even though he had ADHD, but he kept getting into trouble because he couldn't sit still and because he goofed off with his friends in class. When his teacher realized that sitting near his friends made it hard for Scott to pay attention, she changed the seating arrangement, and he no longer got into so much trouble. She also allowed him to sit on a large inflatable ball so that he could gently move around at his desk, which helped him concentrate.

for you to do

Below is a list of problems that many teens with ADHD struggle with. Circle the problems that bother you most.

Having trouble paying attention in class

Finding it hard to sit still

Talking with others during class

Getting bad grades

Handing papers in late

Losing papers

Forgetting homework assignments

Not listening to others

Getting mad at others

Getting into fights

Having temper tantrums

Making careless mistakes

Not finishing schoolwork

Getting distracted

Talking too much

Interrupting others

5

... and more to do

Most likely, your ADHD isn't a problem for you all the time. There are probably times and places where it's worse than others. For example, it may be worse in a classroom where you have to sit for hours on end than it is on a soccer field, where you get to move your body. Let's find out when and where your ADHD symptoms cause you problems.

What is the most severe symptom of ADHD for you?

_____

What situations make this symptom worse?

_____

_____

What situations make this symptom better?

_____

_____

In the situations where your ADHD is most severe, what changes could you make to minimize your symptoms?

_____

_____

How could you try to change your environment to accommodate your symptoms?

_____

_____

defining yourself by what you can do 3

for you to know

Each day you have the choice to define yourself by your strengths or your weaknesses.

One teen with ADHD struggled at school every day. Even in his English class where he tried hardest, he would get bad grades. He began to think he was stupid. All his papers were filled with red marks correcting his spelling and grammar mistakes. He also got into trouble for going out with some friends and coming home drunk. His parents made him go to therapy. He wondered how he would ever be a success in life.

Another teen was good looking, had a lot of friends, was popular with all the girls, and was a star player on the baseball team. His parents were very caring and were able to afford special programs to help him with his schoolwork.

When you read about these two teens, it may seem that one must be miserable and the other has a charmed life. What if you learned that both of these teens are the same person, seen from a different view? You can change how you view yourself by choosing what to focus on: your strengths or your weaknesses.

for you to do

Write about yourself focusing only on your weaknesses. What are you really bad at? What do others say when they complain about you?

_____

_____

_____

_____

_____

Now write about yourself focusing only on your strengths. What are your gifts? What are you naturally good at?

_____

_____

_____

_____

_____

... and more to do

When you are going through your own challenges, you may find yourself thinking that everyone else has it easy compared to you. But all people have challenges and opportunities in their lives.

Think of a person you are jealous of. Can you think of some challenges in that person's life?

_____

_____

_____

Think of a person you feel sorry for. Can you think of some opportunities that person has that many other people don't?

_____

_____

_____

Can you think of some opportunities, talents, skills, or resources you have that make you dazzlingly unique?

_____

_____

_____

4 what went right?

---

for you to know

Teens with ADHD may fall into the trap of asking themselves "Why am I so stupid?" or "Why can't I just keep my mouth shut?" after they get into trouble. Even when something seems to have gone wrong, you have the power to ask positive questions, such as "What went right?" When you ask yourself this type of question, you will start to notice what helps you do well.

When Jonathan got his report card, he had a B in his history class but Cs and Ds in all of his other classes. His mother asked him, "What went right in your history class? How were you able to do so well in that one class?"

Jonathan thought about it and realized that the teacher never gave the class assignments or directions that were not already on their assignment sheets. All his other teachers announced their assignments. Jonathan's parents kept a copy of his history assignment sheets, and they always asked if he had completed specific assignments.

By asking what went right, Jonathan and his parents realized that he could succeed if he had written reminders of every assignment. Jonathan's other teachers agreed to give him his assignments in writing.

for you to do

Describe a success you had recently.

_____

_____

Write three things you did that contributed to this positive outcome.

1. _____

2. _____

3. _____

Describe a problem you're having right now.

_____

_____

How can the three things you did that helped you succeed before help you in the problem you have now?

_____

_____

_____

... and more to do

For each category, tell about something you did right in the last week.

Dating

_____

_____

Schoolwork

_____

_____

Social situations

_____

_____

Family

_____

_____

finding a good match for your skills 5

---

for you to know

People with ADHD have unique sets of interests and skills that they are passionate about. The place where your passion meets your purpose is your "sweet spot." If you live your life from your sweet spot, you can become very successful in life.

Greg struggled with getting organized for school. He had a hard time writing papers, and his grades suffered. One day, while doing Internet research for a paper, he realized that the search engine seemed to work the same way his brain did. Just as his mind leaped from interest to interest based on associations, so did the Internet. He decided he wanted to work in Internet technology as a career. He was so excited by this idea that he started to improve his grades so he could get into a good school to study Internet technology.

for you to do

Write down five qualities that would help people do well in each of these careers. The first one has been done for you as an example.

Hotel concierge:

1. _easy to talk to_

2. _interested in social events_

3. _good at finding information_

4. _organized_

5. _sociable_

Chef

1. _____

2. _____

3. _____

4. _____

5. _____

Auto mechanic

1. _____

2. _____

3. _____

4. _____

5. _____

Hairstylist

1. _____

2. _____

3. _____

4. _____

5. _____

Police officer

1. _____

2. _____

3. _____

4. _____

5. _____

... and more to do

Write down five things that you love to do and are good at.

1. _____

2. _____

3. _____

4. _____

5. _____

List five jobs that match one (or all) of the things you just wrote down.

1. _____

2. _____

3. _____

4. _____

5. _____

Ask your teachers and parents if they know anyone who works in one of the areas you've identified. Then set up a time to meet with that person. During the meeting, you can ask questions like these:

• What do I need to do to prepare for a career in this field?

• What sort of summer job would help me determine if this career is a good match for me?

• What specific interests and talents would I need to succeed in this field?

your personality traits and learning style

6

for you to know

Many of your ADHD symptoms are related to common personality traits and learning styles that are not dysfunctional. You can find out how these traits and learning styles make up your uniqueness and offer specific opportunities in different settings.

Doug came to therapy because he was failing in school. It wasn't because he wasn't smart—in grade school, he had been at the top of the class. When his therapist asked what had changed, Doug said, "This year, all the teachers do is lecture on the same material that's in the book. In middle school, we would break up into groups and debate, and I always did great in those classes." As he and his therapist spoke more about school, Doug realized that he was intelligent and that he learned best when he had to solve problems. With that understanding, Doug was able to gain some confidence in his natural abilities and began to explore what types of careers he could thrive in.

Tyler was also failing in school. His greatest passion was music. He wanted to learn how to play many different instruments. He had even formed his own band, and they performed songs he had written. Tyler's enthusiasm for music fueled his motivation in other arenas, so when his parents told him that they wouldn't pay for his guitar lessons until he raised his grades, he lost interest in school and his grades fell even further. Tyler felt his natural gift of creativity and musical talent was not honored. When he talked to his parents about how music gave him the energy to get through his schoolwork, his parents agreed on a trial basis to fund his lessons. Tyler vowed to work harder in school to show his parents how important his music was to him.

17

for you to do

These traits may be related to ADHD, but they are not disorders or deficits. Circle any that describe you.

Creativity

Imagination

Emotional sensitivity

The need for activity

Excitability

Strong will

Wide-ranging curiosity

Flexibility

Passion

Dreaminess

Sociability

The ability to solve problems

The need for change

Vision

Quickness

A preference for creating structure rather than following it

An innovative mind

Emotional expressiveness

A preference for learning by doing rather than listening

The need for stimulation

As you look over this list, you can see that many of these qualities are highly admirable and could lead to success in many fields. Describe some environments that you or any person with the qualities you circled would be a good match for. For example, leaders like to create structure rather than follow structure. So a person who liked to solve problems in the real world by creating structure might be an excellent leader.

_____

_____

_____

... and more to do

Review the list of traits you circled, and list as many people as you can who share these same traits and are successful or admirable. These might be people you know personally, or public or historical figures, like Thomas Edison and Albert Einstein, who were innovators with wide-ranging curiosity and used their imagination to solve real-world problems. Try to think of ten people who have succeeded not in spite of these traits but because of these traits.

1. _____

2. _____

3. _____

4. _____

5. _____

6. _____

7. _____

8. _____

9. _____

10. _____

7 creating strategies to overcome obstacles

for you to know

Every time you go after something you want, whether it be good grades, a dating relationship, or a spot on the varsity baseball team, you will face obstacles. An obstacle is not a sign to turn around but rather a challenge to figure out how to get past. If you think ahead about the obstacles you might face, you are less likely to be discouraged when they show up.

Stephanie wanted a steady boyfriend. She realized that the obstacle getting in the way of this goal was the fact that she drank too much at parties, which was not helping her attract the kind of guy she was looking for. When she brainstormed what she could do to overcome this obstacle, she realized that the first step was simply to not drink. As she stopped drinking, she started to act more like herself at parties. She found that she made better decisions and was able to start making friends with guys she liked, which eventually led to her finding a boyfriend she really liked.

for you to do

Write down a goal you want to accomplish and three obstacles you might encounter on the way to achieving that goal. Then write down three steps you could take to overcome those obstacles.

Here's an example:

Goal: *To get better grades*

Obstacle: *I never feel like doing my homework*

To overcome this obstacle, I can

1. *call the library homework support line.*

2. *ask my teachers for study tips.*

3. *cut out one hour of watching videos online so I have more time to get my homework done at my own pace.*

Goal: _____

Obstacle 1: _____

To overcome this obstacle, I can

1. _____

2. _____

3. _____

Obstacle 2: _____

To overcome this obstacle, I can

    1. _____

    2. _____

    3. _____

Obstacle 3: _____

To overcome this obstacle, I can

    1. _____

    2. _____

    3. _____

... and more to do

Draw a picture of yourself meeting your goal. Imagine how good you will feel when you achieve your goal.

8 using your goals to motivate you

for you to know

Teens with ADHD can get overwhelmed when they want something but don't know how to make it happen. For example, you might think, "I want to get good grades, but I don't know how." Understanding *how* to achieve a goal is important, but it is also important to understand *why* a particular goal is worthwhile. When you understand why, you can use that goal to motivate you.

Stephen had stopped trying in school. He felt like his teachers picked on him, and he found most of his classes boring, except for biology. But he loved sports, interacting with people, and being active. The one time he'd gone to a physical therapist for an injury, he'd thought it would be a fun job to have. So when one of his teachers asked him what careers he was interested in, he said, "Sports medicine or physical therapy."

His teacher said, "You'd be great in sports medicine. You're so likable, and you could be physically active. You'd be surrounded by athletes and would never have to sit still!" She helped him to see that if he could get good enough grades to go to college and get a degree in physical therapy or sports medicine, he could spend the rest of his life earning money doing what he loved.

For the first time, Stephen realized that he had a reason to pay attention in school. He was motivated to work hard and get good enough grades to go to college.

for you to do

Briefly describe one of your goals.

_____

_____

_____

Just writing down your thoughts can help you start on the path to success, so complete the following statements even if they don't feel quite true for you.

I want to achieve this goal because

_____

_____

If I succeed, I will feel confident that

_____

_____

Three benefits of succeeding in this area are

1. _____

2. _____

3. _____

If I succeed at this, I won't have to deal with

_____

_____

... and more to do

Some of the following goals may not be particularly important to you or may not apply to you; for example, you may already have a boyfriend or girlfriend. Even so, thinking of reasons to succeed is helpful practice, so imagine that you do care about these goals and write down two reasons why you want to succeed at achieving each.

Finding a boyfriend or girlfriend

1. _____

2. _____

Being physically fit and healthy

1. _____

2. _____

Getting into a particular college

1. _____

2. _____

Having friends

1. _____

2. _____

Getting a summer job

1. _____

2. _____

identifying and expressing your feelings

for you to know

One of the best ways to manage your ADHD is by increasing your ability to know what you are feeling, to name your feelings, and then to express them skillfully. The more you can name your feelings in the moment, the better you will be able to cope with them.

When Morgan said she had difficulty doing her homework, her therapist asked her to imagine a recent time when she sat down to do her homework. He said, "What do you feel at that moment when you are trying to get started?"

Morgan thought about it, then said, "I feel insecure and small, like I can't do my homework." She bit her lip and continued, "I feel ... not good enough."

As she voiced these feelings, Morgan realized that they were the main source of her resistance to homework. Her therapist assured her that she could help herself by learning to name and express her feelings in other situations as well.

for you to do

Describe a recent event that upset you.

_____

_____

_____

Name your feelings connected with this event.

_____

Describe three helpful actions you could take to express your feelings when you are upset.

1. _____

2. _____

3. _____

... and more to do

At a time when you are experiencing a negative feeling, like anger or fear, ask yourself, "What am I feeling right now?" Imagine that the feeling you are experiencing is like a wave. Practice watching the wave come and go as you slowly breathe in and out.

What was it like to imagine your feeling this way?

_____

_____

Was it helpful for you to imagine your feeling as a wave? Tell why or why not.

_____

_____

10 taking charge of your thoughts

---

for you to know

You can take charge of what you think. You can categorize your thoughts as helpful—thoughts that give you a boost and make you feel better about yourself—or unhelpful—thoughts that make you feel worse about yourself. Then you can choose to challenge those unhelpful negative thoughts. Think of yourself as a gatekeeper who chooses which thoughts can guide your life and which thoughts get shut out.

Sam had changed schools three times in the last five years. In each school he experienced conflict and failure. As he was preparing to start at a new school that was only for kids with ADHD, he told himself that going there meant he was stupid because he couldn't do well in a regular school.

His counselor helped him to label this thought as unhelpful and suggested that Sam replace it with some helpful thoughts; for example, he would finally be going to a school that would understand his learning style.

Sam realized that choosing to focus on the helpful thought helped him be more enthusiastic about going to the new school. In turn, his enthusiasm would help him do better than he would have otherwise.

for you to do

Below are four common negative thoughts that many teens with ADHD struggle with. Under each thought, write two alternative positive thoughts. One has been done for you as an example.

"Having ADHD means I'm not as smart as the other kids."

1. *The harder I work, the more I can build my brain.*

2. *ADHD means I have a difference that can be an advantage. I'm a better debater because I think on my feet more quickly.*

"Why should I try? I'll only fail."

1. _____

2. _____

"I don't need to study hard; I don't want to go to college anyway."

1. _____

2. _____

"Why should I listen to my parents? All they do is criticize me."

1. _____

2. _____

On an index card, write down all the helpful thoughts you were able to create. Carry the card with you and read it each time you need to feel a boost of motivation.

... and more to do

Choose a specific problem you have. Write down all your current thoughts—both helpful and unhelpful—about this problem.

_____

_____

_____

_____

Now go back and mark each helpful thought with a star and each unhelpful thought with an X.

Write down two new empowering thoughts about this problem.

_____

_____

As you begin to choose the empowering thoughts and challenge the disempowering thoughts, notice how this changes your problem. Write down any changes you notice.

_____

_____

_____

---

for you to know

It's not true that there are smart people and not-so-smart people and that those labels never change. Just like in sports, where you can build your muscles and skills, in school you can build your intelligence by trying harder—you can be a brain athlete! Understanding this idea can help you replace the negative thought "Why should I study? My ADHD makes it too hard" with this positive one: "The more I study, the more I build my brain!"

Christopher was well behaved in school but he thought it was so boring that he didn't pay attention in class and was far behind others in his reading and writing skills.

One of his teachers told him that he could build his brain by trying harder. She said, "The harder you work, Christopher, the more you can rewire your brain to make you better at reading and writing. Don't worry about what the other kids can do; just think about building your own brain."

Christopher wasn't exactly sure how to start building his brain, so he asked his teacher what she meant. She explained, "You've fallen behind in reading, and that probably makes your schoolwork frustrating. Why don't you try reading a book you're really interested in, even if it's below your grade level? That will help you build your capacity to pay attention without getting so frustrated."

So Christopher spent a half hour each day reading one of the Harry Potter books. After a while, he had not only built up his reading skills but also increased his ability to concentrate. It became much easier for him to pay attention in class.

for you to do

What skill would you like to build? It could be anything, from remembering details of the book you're reading to solving math problems.

_____

What specific activity could you do every day for fifteen minutes to build that skill?

_____

Challenge yourself to spend one week where you practice this new activity for fifteen minutes a day. Write down the obstacles you might run into.

_____

_____

_____

How could you overcome these obstacles?

_____

_____

_____

List three action steps you can take in order to practice this new skill for fifteen minutes a day.

1. _____

2. _____

3. _____

... and more to do

Tell how you will feel if you follow through on your commitment to build this new skill.

_____

_____

_____

_____

_____

12 listening when you feel like you can't

for you to know

It can be very hard for teens with ADHD to listen to others, but not listening may cause many problems for you. You can build your listening "muscles" by practicing listening without interruption for five minutes at a time. When you get good at that, you can practice in different situations or increase the amount of time you listen without interruption.

Hannah didn't listen to her parents because she thought they were always repeating themselves. Her mom and dad were often angry with her for being inattentive, so she asked her therapist what she could do about it. Her therapist suggested that she start by listening carefully with full attention for a small amount of time. As she got better at it, she could gradually increase the amount of time.

The first time Hannah did this, she was amazed at how much her parents appreciated seeing that she was listening. She also happened to be paying attention when her dad reminded her to bring her science project to school, which helped her not lose points in class that day. She was surprised at how such a small effort—just five minutes—could make such a noticeable change in her life.

Her therapist also suggested that Hannah try pretending she was an investigative reporter who had to find answers to the five Ws—who, what, where, when, and why—as she listened to others. Rather than being bored by others, Hannah challenged herself to figure out the details as if she had to report them to someone else. In class, when her teacher gave out instructions or assignments, she no longer tuned out. Instead, she would make sure she fully understood what the teacher was saying; if she didn't, she would ask questions to get clarity.

for you to do

For five minutes, practice listening to someone who typically complains that you don't pay attention during conversations. Make sure that you have a watch or that there's a clock you can see as you engage in conversation. Write down the name of a person you can practice this with.

_____

After you have practiced, respond to these questions:

What did you notice about yourself as you tried to listen?

_____

_____

_____

Was listening harder or easier to do than you expected? Tell why.

_____

_____

_____

What did you notice about the other person's reaction? Did the conversation go differently than it usually does?

_____

_____

_____

... and more to do

Now that you've practiced listening for a specific length of time, try listening with the goal of gathering specific information. As you listen, ask yourself: Who? What? Where? When? Why?

After you have practiced, respond to these questions:

What did you notice about yourself as you tried to listen?

_____

_____

_____

Was gathering the information harder or easier than you thought it would be? Tell why.

_____

_____

_____

What did you notice about the other person's reaction? Did the conversation go differently than it usually does?

_____

_____

_____

for you to know

You can gain control over your hyperactivity by simply noticing it and observing it rather than being driven by it. This approach of taking a step back and witnessing your behavior without judging or criticizing yourself is called mindfulness. The more you are mindful of your activity level, the better chance you have of calming yourself down.

David often got into fights with his parents because he didn't do his chores when he was asked. One Saturday morning, his mother exclaimed in frustration, "David, why is it so hard for you to follow simple instructions!"

When David thought about it, he realized that folding his laundry and doing the dishes were so slow paced that it was hard for him to calm down enough to complete the tasks. He felt almost as if he were being driven by a motor, and he could not tolerate the boredom of his chores.

He explained this feeling to his mom and found that just talking about it with her was helpful. She suggested that if he could just notice he was feeling hyperactive but choose to do the task anyway, he could make his life a lot easier.

After that, David stopped blustering about avoiding the tedious tasks. Instead, he would say to himself, "I notice how hyperactive I feel, but it will be much easier to just get this task done so my mom will get off my back."

for you to do

Choose a calm, quiet place where you can sit or lie down comfortably. Adjust yourself so your head and back are aligned and supported. Mentally scan your body, using words like "tight," "loose," "heavy," or "warm" to describe what you notice. Start with your head, and notice if you feel any tension in your scalp, eyes, nose, or mouth. Just notice what you are sensing, without judging it in any way. Move your attention down through your neck, shoulders, arms, and hands. Scan your chest and stomach area, down through your pelvis and bottom. Continue down your legs to your feet.

When you are done, write down any sensations you noticed.

_____

_____

Did you feel any hyperactivity in your body? If so, where did you feel it? Describe what your hyperactivity feels like as best you can. Does it feel like an engine revving up or like butterflies, or is it a different feeling altogether?

_____

_____

On a scale from 1 to 10, how intense would you rate the level of hyperactivity, with 1 being very still and 10 being extremely hyper? _____

Now that you have practiced in a quiet setting, try to notice your hyperactivity as you go through your day. You don't have to lie down or scan your entire body; just ask yourself what your level of hyperactivity is and where you feel it.

On a scale from 1 to 10, rate your level of hyperactivity in these settings:

_____ In the morning as you are getting ready for school

_____ In your first class

_____ At lunchtime

_____ In your most difficult class

_____ In your easiest class

_____ In a social situation

_____ When you are trying to do your homework

... and more to do

Below are some descriptions you can use to practice noticing when you are hyperactive.

- I notice I'm feeling more revved up.

- I notice how hard it is to sit still.

- I notice that I feel like blurting out what's on my mind.

- I notice that I feel like moving around.

Write your own sentences that will help you accept and witness your hyperactivity rather than be driven by it.

_____

_____

_____

_____

pushing back against your "can'ts" 14

for you to know

When you tell yourself "I can't," you decrease your motivation and are less likely to take charge of your life. By challenging yourself when you notice yourself saying "I can't," you can change what happens.

Mike got mostly Cs and Ds in his freshman year. When he started his sophomore year, he told himself, "I can't be a good student." His school counselor asked him to imagine what his reaction would be if someone else came up to him and told him he couldn't be a good student. Mike realized that he would get really mad and tell the person that he could do better if he tried harder.

As he began to set goals for himself, he found there were other "can'ts" that had to be challenged. He thought, "I can't study for more than a half hour a night." He worked with his counselor to challenge this idea and realized that he was capable of studying for three or more hours each night if he needed to. He also told himself, "I can't pay attention in math class; it's so boring." Again he practiced challenging this idea and recognized that although it might not be fun or easy, he could pay attention in his math class.

By getting in the habit of challenging his self-defeating beliefs, Mike was able to change his behavior, and the outcome was that he improved his grades.

for you to do

Describe a situation where you doubt yourself.

_____

_____

Now write down four ways you can challenge this idea.

1. _____

2. _____

3. _____

4. _____

List four resources that could make it easier to do what you thought you could not do.

1. _____

2. _____

3. _____

4. _____

List four action steps you can take to make it easier to do what you doubted you could do.

1. _____

2. _____

3. _____

4. _____

... and more to do

Below are common statements of self-doubt that ADHD teens say to themselves. Read each one and write a challenging statement that changes it from an "I can't" to an "I can."

I can't study as much as other kids.

_____

_____

I can't pay attention in class.

_____

_____

I can't take tests.

_____

_____

15 ending the blame game

---

for you to know

When you are feeling hurt in a relationship, blaming the other person for the problems usually makes it harder to repair the relationship. Even if the other person is in part responsible for hurting you, blaming almost always makes things worse. Instead, focus on how you are contributing to the problem. You can't change the other person, but you can change your own behavior.

Jennifer's feelings were hurt when her boyfriend, Kevin, didn't return her text messages right away. He also tended to study a lot, and she worried he was just using schoolwork as an excuse to avoid her. She was thinking about breaking up with him.

Her older sister helped her see that she was blaming most of the problems in the relationship on Kevin. Jennifer realized that she played a role in the problems because she felt insecure and tended not to tell Kevin how she felt.

Once she understood how she contributed to their problems, she was able to talk more honestly with Kevin. She told him that she felt worried that he was avoiding her and that she would like to spend more time with him.

for you to do

Describe a relationship problem where your feelings are hurt.

_____

_____

_____

Tell how the other person is to blame.

_____

_____

_____

List all the benefits of blaming the other person for your hurt feelings.

_____

_____

_____

List the costs of blaming the other person for your hurt feelings.

_____

_____

_____

Describe how your own behavior contributes to the problem.

_____

_____

_____

activity 15 ✳ ending the blame game

... and more to do

Using the same situation you just described, write your complaint about the other person in one short sentence.

_____

_____

Now translate your complaint into a specific request.

_____

_____

Practice using requests in your relationships rather than complaints.

learning from your jealousy 16

---

for you to know

Many teens with ADHD feel jealous of their peers who don't seem to struggle as much as they do. If you are driven by jealousy of someone else, you are letting your thoughts about that person control your emotional state. Remind yourself that your chances of reaching your goals improve if you remain in charge of your own emotional state.

Paul felt jealousy toward some of his friends who did well in school and seemed to do it easily. Whenever he talked to his mom about how easy all his friends had it, she would remind him to tell himself "seemingly," as in "John has it easy, seemingly." She encouraged him to use this word each time he felt jealous of someone else. She told him, "Everyone has challenges. We never really know how hard or easy it is for other people, because we all try to hide our struggles and shame."

When Paul made it a habit to use the word "seemingly" every time he felt jealous, he realized he could measure his progress by seeing how close he was getting to his own goals rather than comparing himself to others.

for you to do

In every stage of life, there will always be people who seem to have more than you and people who seem to have less than you. Tell how your life would be different if you let go of comparing yourself to others to determine how well you're doing.

_____

_____

_____

_____

What other method can you use to determine your level of progress? For example, you can set a goal and measure your progress by how close you come to that goal rather than by comparing yourself to others.

_____

_____

_____

_____

When you find yourself feeling jealous of someone, make it a habit to ask yourself, "Do I really want this person to create negative emotions for me?"

... and more to do

You can use your jealousy to clarify your own goals and to find useful strategies.

Write down the three things that make you the most jealous.

1. _____

2. _____

3. _____

For each one, write a goal that brings this quality into your own life but allows you to measure yourself by your own progress rather than in comparison to someone else.

1. _____

2. _____

3. _____

Challenge yourself to ask someone you are jealous of for specific tips on how that person succeeds. Write down the response you get.

_____

_____

_____

_____

17 are you normal?

for you to know

A leading source of stress for teens is wondering "Am I normal?" So it is perfectly normal for you to wonder if you are normal. Belonging to a group that shares your passions is one way to help yourself feel normal.

Mark was embarrassed about some of the accommodations he received at school. Sometimes when the person who took notes for him arrived in class, his teacher would let Mark know. At times like that, Mark was very worried what other kids would think.

At other times, he was completely comfortable with the kids around him and didn't worry about being teased. For example, he had a sense of belonging in band, where others knew he had ADHD and accepted him as he was. It was very helpful to him to have a group of friends who were as passionate about music as he was and with whom he didn't feel he had anything to hide.

for you to do

Describe a situation where you were worried if you were normal.

_____

_____

_____

Describe a group of people who would think you were normal in this situation.

_____

_____

_____

List the different social groups you belong to, whether at school, in sports, in your neighborhood, through religious affiliation, or elsewhere.

_____

_____

_____

_____

_____

Draw a circle around the groups where you feel the most normal. Then draw a rectangle around the groups where you question if you are normal.

... and more to do

If you are still seeking a group where you feel you belong, write a list of your interests.

_____

_____

_____

_____

_____

Write three actions steps you could take to find and get involved with a group that shares your interests.

1. _____

2. _____

3. _____

changing your breathing, changing your mood 18

for you to know

The quickest way to change your mood is to change your breathing. Simply by focusing on your breathing you can halt a cascade of inner events that cause anxiety and stress, both of which reduce your capacity to pay attention.

Thomas's struggles with test taking had created a new problem—test anxiety. His school counselor taught him a few simple breathing exercises. One that he found easiest to use was to breathe in to a count of three, then out to a count of three. He used this exercise every day whether he had a test or not.

After a few weeks of practicing his breathing techniques daily, Thomas noticed that he felt much less anxious. He decided that he would practice his breathing before every test to allow him to focus and concentrate as well as possible. It even helped him when he felt anxious during a test.

for you to do

Imagine yourself in a situation that makes you anxious. As you think about this situation, rate your level of anxiety using a scale of 1 to 10, with 1 being deeply relaxed and 10 being extremely anxious.

_____

Practice the following steps:

1. Focus your attention on your breath. Notice if it is quick or slow, shallow or deep.

2. Breathe in so that your stomach rises, taking the breath all the way into your belly. This is called abdominal breathing. If your shoulders are rising as you breathe, relax them.

3. Continue breathing in and count to three.

4. Exhale for a count of three. Continue to practice this conscious breathing for two minutes.

On a scale of 1 to 10, with 1 being deeply relaxed and 10 being extremely anxious, rate your level of anxiety again.

_____

Did you notice any change in your level of anxiety? If so, write about what changes you noticed.

_____

_____

_____

_____

... and more to do

Experiment with the following breathing practice that can help you increase your attention by reducing stress and anxiety. Pay attention to your breathing. Each time you breathe out, say to yourself, "calm and focused."

Tell how this practice affected you.

_____

_____

_____

What did you find helpful about it?

_____

_____

_____

19 what you can do about worry

Daniel worried about many things, including his grades, his friends, and his family. Daniel's therapist told him that almost half of kids with ADHD struggle with anxiety in addition to their ADHD. In talking to his therapist, Daniel began to realize that time spent worrying disrupted his attention, making it more difficult for him to focus, concentrate, or get to sleep. He learned that he couldn't control all the things he worried about, but he could control how much he worried. He realized that as long as he made a note of what actions he could take to address his worries, he could let go of them more easily.

for you to do

Describe a worry that bothers you a lot.

_____

_____

_____

Are there any benefits to worrying about this issue? List them here:

_____

_____

_____

Are there any problems created by worrying about this issue? List them here:

_____

_____

_____

Write down any steps you can take to solve the problem you are worried about.

_____

_____

_____

... and more to do

Try out these ways to let go of your worries and notice which works best for you.

- Imagine your worry in a helium balloon floating off into space.

- Write your worry on a piece of paper, then crumple the paper and throw it away.

- Every time you find yourself worrying about something you've already done as much as you can to solve, ask yourself, "Do I want to get all worked up about this or just let it go for now?"

---

for you to know

Like many teens, you may feel shame about your parents' problems, like divorce, frequent arguments, addictions, or financial troubles. It's important to realize that you did not cause these problems, you cannot control them, and you cannot cure them. The more you can separate yourself from family problems, the more you will be able to focus on organizing your own life.

In addition to struggling with ADHD, James tried to solve many of the problems in his family. After his parents divorced, he noticed that his mom was drinking a lot. He spent a lot of time trying to help her and to figure out how he could get her to stop drinking. The more he got involved in trying to solve her problems, the more his grades fell and the less time he spent with friends. His therapist told him that people with ADHD often spend too much time trying to take care of other people, people who should be taking care of themselves. The other person's life becomes yet another distraction, making it difficult for a teen with ADHD to set and work toward his own goals.

After James joined a support group, he realized that he couldn't control his mother's drinking. He no longer stayed home at night to keep his mom company so she wouldn't drink. He also started talking to his dad about his own needs rather than only about what his mom was doing, and he went to a school counselor to stay on track with figuring out his own goals.

As James got support for moving forward with his own life, his schoolwork and social life improved.

for you to do

Describe a family problem that makes it difficult for you to focus on your own goals.

_____

_____

_____

_____

Write down three things you could do differently to help you separate yourself from the troubling situation.

1. _____

2. _____

3. _____

... and more to do

Write about what your life might be like if you believe you have to control and cure the problems in your family.

_____

_____

_____

_____

_____

Now imagine that you are compassionate about the problems in your family and involved in realistically helpful ways, but that you can separate yourself from the problems you cannot control or cure. Describe what your life could be like.

_____

_____

_____

_____

21 how to get high without drugs or alcohol

for you to know

Many teens with ADHD seek stimulation. Like them, you may crave excitement and constantly be looking for more action and more intense experiences. This trait may make experimenting with drugs and alcohol a very real temptation. You can safely honor your need for thrills by finding healthy and natural methods for gaining positive emotional "highs."

William was a skilled and fierce competitor on the soccer field. He was used to the cheering of the crowds and the rush of adrenaline it brought him. When he had to give up competitive soccer because of an injury, he found himself deeply unsettled and craving more and more excitement in his life.

He had experimented with smoking pot and found that it did settle his feeling of being on the prowl for something new and thrilling. However, he didn't like the feeling of being out of control and decided he wouldn't do that again.

After smelling pot on him, his parents sent him to therapy to get him some help. His therapist honored his need for stimulation, and they worked on a plan for finding natural "highs" in his life. While William couldn't play competitive soccer, he could do many other activities. He found that hiking was exciting for him, and he loved being out in nature and getting a chance to challenge himself. He found that extreme weather heightened his outdoor experience. Hiking also gave him the excuse to explore new areas. His newfound sense of adventure helped him fulfill his need for intense activity and excitement.

for you to do

Create a list of activities that are intense and exciting that you would like to try.

_____   _____

_____   _____

_____   _____

_____   _____

Here are some activities you may not have thought of but might be interested in trying. Circle the ones you would like to experiment with.

Yoga	Spiritual retreats
Live music concerts	Rock climbing
Ice skating	Exploring new parts of your community
Hiking	Taking a class in something you've never tried before
Biking	
Frisbee	Amusement parks
Dancing	Joining a group that shares an interest of yours
Meditation	Finding local festivals

... and more to do

Write down three concrete steps you can take to try a new activity.

1. _____

2. _____

3. _____

taking a stand against peer pressure 22

---

for you to know

One of the great gifts of ADHD—imagination—can make some teens more "suggestible" and therefore at risk for giving in to peer pressure. On the flip side, the "defiance" of ADHD can be channeled to stand up to peer pressure. You can notice your personal pitfalls and internal strengths to prepare in advance for peer pressure.

Amanda's friends were going to spend Saturday night at a local beach. The route to the beach was fairly treacherous, and Amanda was worried that if the people she drove with were drinking, it could be dangerous getting home. She thought back to earlier that summer when some kids from her school had been cited by a police officer for building a campfire on the beach; many of them had also been arrested for underage drinking. When she voiced her concerns to her friends, they assured her that things would be different this time; they had learned their lesson from the last event where lots of people got busted.

She had almost decided to go to the beach when her defiant side kicked in. Amanda said to herself, "This is silly. It's just one night out of many, and there are so many risks that I won't even have fun." She boldly told her friends that it wasn't worth the risks to her and that she would be going to the movies with some friends instead.

for you to do

If your friends are doing something you know is risky, what do they say to urge you to follow along?

_____

_____

_____

_____

Use your imagination to come up with responses to what your friends might say.

_____

_____

_____

_____

... and more to do

Put a check mark next to the strengths you have that help you stand up to peer pressure.

☐ I'm an original thinker.

☐ I'm defiant.

☐ I don't go along with the crowd.

☐ I'm not afraid to speak my mind.

☐ I think quickly enough to come up with good retorts.

☐ I have good ideas for safer alternative activities.

List any other strengths you notice in yourself that help you resist peer pressure.

_____

_____

_____

_____

What are the positive consequences of resisting peer pressure?

_____

_____

_____

_____

23 gaining confidence

for you to know

You don't have to be perfect to be confident. You can create confidence by defining yourself by your talents rather than your failings, by making a practice of noticing what you like about yourself, and by giving yourself credit for handling difficult situations rather than being ashamed of your personal struggles.

Sean wasn't able to talk with girls like the other guys did. Not only was he shy, but he also felt like he wasn't good looking. When he got up the courage to talk to a girl in class, he would just ask questions about the homework instead of starting a more personal conversation. Then he would beat himself up for not being more forward or acting more interested.

When Sean noticed that it took a lot of courage for him to even talk with girls, he decided that more practice would help him open up over time. He admitted how difficult it was for him and started giving himself credit for trying to overcome his shyness.

for you to do

Write down ten things you think you handled well today.

_____   _____

_____   _____

_____   _____

_____   _____

_____   _____

Describe a personal struggle that has been bothering you this last week.

_____

_____

_____

What have you criticized yourself for in regard to this struggle?

_____

_____

_____

What did you do well in the face of this personal challenge?

_____

_____

_____

... and more to do

Below are some sentences you can practice saying each day. You may have to actively search for reasons to use these sentences, but challenge yourself to send an encouraging message to yourself ten times every day.

"I like how I did that."

"I'm really gaining momentum."

"That wasn't easy, and it took a lot of strength for me to do it."

"If I keep at it, the sky is the limit."

for you to know

Developing an independent identity is part of a teenager's job. It is normal for teens to challenge parents as part of defining who they are and how they are different from their parents. You can stay connected to your family even during times when you challenge their values, beliefs, or interests. You can even use your conflict to gain greater intimacy and support.

Alex's parents were hoping he would earn a scholarship to college because he was such a good tennis player. They offered him lots of support and encouragement to be the best he could be. But to Alex, their encouragement just felt like pressure, and he began to resent the intense dedication and practice it took to be at the top of his game. He wanted more time to be with friends and more free time.

When he realized how angry he was with his parents, he finally decided to explain how he felt. He said, "I feel pressured by your expectations. I want to play, but I want have fun with it and also have a social life."

At first, there was disappointment and anger on both sides. However, as the conversation went on, Alex's parents began to see that it was healthy for Alex to want a more balanced life and that their pressure was making it difficult for him to be clear about what he really wanted since it felt like it was limiting his freedom. As his parents began to see the situation from his side, Alex was able to express his gratitude for their support. Together, they all agreed that he would scale back the intensity of his tennis schedule.

for you to do

Describe a conflict you have with your parents.

_____

_____

_____

_____

Describe the problem from your parents' perspective.

_____

_____

_____

_____

What do your parents need to know about you to see it from your side?

_____

_____

_____

_____

… and more to do

Write three specific requests you would like to make of your parents.

_____

_____

_____

At a time when everyone is calm and able to listen, have a conversation with your parents where you show respect for their perspective. During this conversation, make specific requests rather than complaining.

25 handling criticism

for you to know

You can translate criticism into coaching. Sometimes adults give feedback in ways that hurt more than help, but you can take charge and learn to find positive direction and guidance in criticism.

Daniel was really hurt when his mom told him that one of his teachers had said he was uncooperative with authority and seemed unfriendly with his peers. He admitted that he had a hard time getting along with this teacher but then said, "I think she's picking on me. I'm not like that with every teacher."

"What about being friendly with the other kids?" his mom asked.

Daniel thought about it for a moment. "Well, I'm often in a bad mood because I have such a hard time trying to concentrate. Maybe that's why I seem unfriendly."

His mom suggested that they try to translate this criticism into specific action steps to help Daniel. The two of them met with Daniel's teacher to come up with ways to solve each problem rather than have it turn into personal conflict. Through these conversations, his teacher came to understand that Daniel wasn't being actively defiant; he was simply unable to follow directions in some cases. And rather than ignoring his peers when he was trying to concentrate, Daniel learned to say, "Sorry, I can't talk right now. I'm trying really hard to stay focused."

for you to do

Write down a criticism about yourself that you hear frequently.

_____

_____

_____

Now imagine the same message coming from a beloved coach who wants to see you do better. What would that message be?

_____

_____

_____

... and more to do

Write down three action steps you could do this week to help you to follow the guidance from this coaching message.

_____

_____

_____

for you to know

Your success in school is directly related to how much time you put in studying. Students who do better than you are not necessarily smarter than you; they may simply be logging in more hours of study time. Many teens prefer to do their schoolwork on weekdays and Sundays, but "Study on Saturday" can become your mantra for telling yourself to go the extra mile.

It was the day of Dylan's final exam in his class on U.S. presidents. After the test, he was shocked to find out that almost everyone in the class had memorized not only their major achievements but also the exact dates each president served. Dylan had just assumed that memorizing the specific dates would take so much time that it wasn't a reasonable area for the test to cover. He was wrong.

Dylan asked some other kids how much time they had spent studying for the exam and how they had fit in the time. He found out that most had spent at least ten hours studying for this one final exam and that, in addition to studying weekdays, they logged in long hours on Saturdays before finals. Dylan realized that he had lowered the bar on what he expected from himself.

for you to do

How many hours do you spend studying each week?

_____

Ask some friends you admire for their good grades how many hours they spend studying each week. Write down their answers here.

_____

What goals do you have for yourself in schoolwork?

_____

_____

How many extra hours would you need to study to achieve your goals?

_____

... and more to do

Using a weekly calendar, fill in how you usually spend your time. Look to see where you can add the additional hours of studying you would need to meet your schoolwork goals.

Write down your plan here:

_____

_____

_____

_____

_____

_____

27 the power of fifteen minutes a day

for you to know

In just fifteen minutes a day, you can strengthen skills that will help you reach your goals. For example, if you want to be more organized, you can make dramatic changes by spending fifteen minutes a day straightening your room. If you want to increase your physical fitness, you can begin by exercising for fifteen minutes a day. You can start small and build momentum as you go along.

Anthony's biggest problem was that he was so disorganized, he never could find his work or remember when his projects were due. He showed up to classes without the right books and materials, and he lost many of his assignment sheets and other organizers. He decided to spend fifteen minutes a day answering the following questions:

- *What projects are due this week?*

- *What do I need for school today?*

- *What is my study plan for today?*

- *Did I complete my study plan yesterday?*

By taking the time to organize his day and create a plan, Anthony became more organized and had more success in school.

for you to do

Write down one new skill you would like to develop.

_____

Review your weekly schedule. For each day, what is the best time to take fifteen minutes to build this new skill?

Monday	Tuesday	Wednesday	Thursday	Friday	Saturday	Sunday

Make a commitment to practice your new skill for fifteen minutes each day. Do not let yourself go longer than fifteen minutes in the first month. If you push yourself harder, you might lose the motivation that comes from knowing that however difficult the practice is, it will be over quickly.

... and more to do

It's likely that there will be times when you feel like skipping your practice. If that happens, you can use these messages to talk back to the discouraging voice that tells you to just skip it.

- "I can do anything for just fifteen minutes."

- "I'll feel so good when I've finished my fifteen minutes."

- "I can improve my life if I make this small investment of time every single day."

- "I have the strength to keep this commitment to myself."

Write your own responses to the discouraging self-talk.

_____

_____

_____

failing your way to success 28

---

for you to know

Every failure is feedback. Instead of feeling defeated, you can choose to view a failure as a chance to gain information and build resilience, skills, and problem-solving abilities.

Neha was afraid of getting rejected at colleges her friends might get into. She decided to apply mostly to safe schools and to only one school that was extremely competitive. While she did get into one of her safe schools, she was rejected from the one competitive school she applied to. She felt like a failure.

As she talked about it with others, Neha realized that she would have applied to many other colleges if she hadn't been so afraid of failure. She also realized that she was able to bounce back after the failure; it didn't crush her.

After her freshman year of college, Neha decided to transfer. By then, she knew that she could handle rejection letters, and she applied to as many competitive schools as safe schools. This time, she got into a highly competitive school, though once again she was rejected from several top-tier colleges.

Neha had learned that by not being afraid of failure she increased the possibilities open to her.

for you to do

Describe a recent failure experience that is still bothering you.

_____

_____

_____

On a scale of 1 (not bothered) to 10 (extremely bothered), rate how upsetting this is to you. _____

Put a check mark next to any of these lessons you learned from this failure experience.

☐ I need to gain skills in being respectful to others.

☐ I need to work harder to get the grades I want.

☐ Cheating isn't worth it.

☐ I can ask someone for the information I need to succeed.

☐ Instead of getting angry, I can talk with other people to gain perspective.

Write down other lessons you may have learned from this experience.

_____

_____

_____

How could you do things differently next time you are in a similar situation?

_____

_____

_____

... and more to do

What are some things you would do in your life if you were not afraid of failure?

_____

_____

_____

Challenge yourself to collect five rejections this week. You might ask people for help, ask a friend to study with you, ask for a date, apply to jobs you might not think you can get, or try out for a talent show.

Seek out as many opportunities as you can to get rejected. You can learn not to take it personally. Sometimes failing simply teaches you that you can bounce back from failure.

for you to know

You might face more disappointments because of your learning difference, but that doesn't mean you have to lower your goals for yourself. You can choose to be bigger than your disappointments and keep going. Many kids with ADHD succeed in school and other arenas, and many adults with ADHD have gone on to be very successful.

In school, getting the one correct answer is sometimes applauded. Beyond school, generating innovative solutions to enormously complex problems can become a matter of life and death. Take, for example, a firefighter with ADHD. He gets to be very active, and his job is definitely not boring. Many of the things that got him into trouble in school have become the very things that help him succeed as a firefighter. When a firefighter arrives on the scene of a fire, there is no correct answer at the back of the book. He needs to work closely with other firefighters to generate many plausible strategies and then decide which one is the best. His ability to see solutions helps him save lives each time there is a crisis.

for you to do

Think of another teen you know who has ADHD and has achieved something you are impressed with. Ask what that person did to overcome ADHD and write the answer here:

_____

_____

_____

Ask for three specific tips for gaining confidence even when you have ADHD and write them down.

1. _____

2. _____

3. _____

Ask your parents or other people you know if they can put you in touch with a successful adult who has ADHD. (Research suggesting that ADHD is genetic is compelling, so there is a good chance that someone in your family has ADHD.) Ask that adult what he or she did to overcome ADHD and write the answer here:

_____

_____

_____

Again, ask for three specific tips for gaining confidence even when you have ADHD and write them down.

1. _____

2. _____

3. _____

... and more to do

After asking questions of successful people with ADHD, what reactions do you have?

_____

_____

_____

_____

_____

Imagine it is five years from now, and someone asks you how you overcame your ADHD. What would you say?

_____

_____

_____

_____

_____

for you to know

Many teens with ADHD feel ashamed to have a diagnosis that makes them different. You can face the feelings that you are different and begin to challenge the idea that differences make you less than others.

Maria wondered why her interests were so different from most other kids'. While they spent a lot of time talking about music or movies, she preferred to go home after school and draw designs for a fashion line she imagined. She knew she wanted to be a designer and liked to use her afternoons to practice.

She decided that rather than trying to pretend she shared the same interests as the others, she would let them know about her main interest. When she brought some of her sketches to school, she found that other kids wanted to see them and were impressed with her talent. She was very happy to learn that they saw the time she spent in drawing not as a weird interest that made her different but as a unique talent in itself.

for you to do

Describe something you try to hide about yourself because you think it makes you different from others.

_____

_____

_____

Write a sentence that translates this difference into an acceptable, easy-to-understand quality that makes you unique. For example, if you prefer small get-togethers to parties, you might write, "I'm more introverted, so I'd rather spend weekends hanging out with a few friends."

_____

_____

_____

How does this translation make you feel compared to the feeling of shame about being different?

_____

_____

_____

... and more to do

Imagine someone who would see the very difference that you are ashamed of as a unique quality about you. What might someone who appreciated the difference in this way say to you?

_____

_____

_____

_____

_____

31 focusing on where you want to go

for you to know

In each moment, you can choose to focus on where you want to go or to dwell on what's not working in your life. The more you focus on what you want for yourself, the better the life you can create for yourself.

Rachel knew she wanted to become a teacher and needed a master's degree to do that, but she had ADHD and found it very hard to take tests. When she did poorly on her SATs, she got discouraging feedback from her school counselor and other people around her. Still, she kept herself focused on becoming a teacher. She went to junior college and with determination did very well. Because of her hard work, she was able to go on to a four-year school that had an excellent education department. Along the way she built up her study skills, motivation, and confidence. She was accepted into a master's program in her field of interest.

Rachel never lost hope because of her test scores. She kept moving forward and figuring out what she had to do to get to the next level.

for you to do

Have you given up on a dream because of a failure experience or a disappointment? If so, describe your dream below.

_____

_____

_____

Tell what makes you doubt your ability to achieve that goal.

_____

_____

_____

Can you think of an alternate route to achieving your goal? Write it here. If you can't think of another route, ask friends, siblings, or parents for help.

_____

_____

_____

If you still think you cannot achieve your goal, describe the essence of what you wanted from that goal. For example, if you asked someone out on a date and were turned down because that person was already in a relationship, you might describe the essence of what you wanted as a caring dating relationship with someone you respect and are attracted to.

_____

_____

_____

... and more to do

Review what you wrote about an alternate route to your goal or the essence of the goal you wanted to achieve. What are three actions you can take this week to move toward your goal?

1. _____

2. _____

3. _____

for you to know

People with ADHD often find it difficult to be organized, but organization is a skill you can build over time. Like a person who breaks a leg might use crutches as a tool, you can develop organizational tools to help you succeed.

Alexis had a hard time managing her schedule and commitments. She often forgot about project due dates, homework assignments, tests, and sports practices. At the start of the new school year, her mother offered to show her how to use a time-management software program for organizing her calendar and to-do lists. Alexis thought it would be really boring to learn the program, but her mother said it would require only a small investment in time and would save her lots of problems. At first, her mom continued to remind her, but over time Alexis learned the system and was able to keep on top of her schedule by herself.

Kirk never threw anything away. He had piles of stuff everywhere, and his backpack was full of papers that were long outdated. His older brother Kyle offered to be an organizational buddy. Kyle helped Kirk realize he couldn't possibly read all the sports magazines he had saved over many years, believing that he would get to them someday; he never even read the newest one because he was so overwhelmed by the mess. With this new understanding, Kirk threw away piles and piles of old magazines and committed to making a dent in his other piles by throwing away five things every single day.

Kyle's next suggestion was that Kirk create a command center for his schoolwork. So Kirk bought an inexpensive bookcase, a small sports-themed trash basket, and a dry-erase board with a pen. On the bookshelf, he put magazine holders labeled with his class names and sports activities. He put all the material for each class and sport in its own holder. He put the trash basket next to the bookcase so that he could easily throw away outdated material. And every evening, he wrote his schedule and to-do list for the next day on the dry-erase board.

for you to do

These tools can help you organize your work and schedule. Circle any that you haven't tried yet and put a star next to the ones you think would help you most.

A software program, like Microsoft Outlook

A cell-phone calendar

Laptop pop-up reminders

A filing system

A day planner

A wall calendar

An online calendar you can sync with other family members

A command center for schoolwork

File drawers

Shelving and bookcases

Stacking trays

Drawer organizers

This week, try out one or more of these tools. You might take a trip to an office supply store to see what appeals to you.

... and more to do

If it's hard for you to spend the time learning or finding the right tools for organization, dig a little deeper. Put a check mark next to any thoughts that stop you from moving forward with organization. Use the blank lines to add your own thoughts.

☐ It takes too much time to learn how to use an online calendar.

☐ Once I get it started, I'll forget all about it.

☐ I can't throw things out because I might need them someday.

☐ I can't throw things out because I need to hold on to the memories in them.

☐ Getting organized is going to take time away from doing my homework.

☐ _____

☐ _____

Write a challenge to each statement that is limiting your progress in organization. For example, if you are keeping things because of the memories, you might write: "I could enjoy the present more if I weren't hanging on to all this stuff."

_____

_____

_____

_____

_____

33 risky behaviors

for you to know

One of the main symptoms of ADHD is impulsiveness—the tendency to act without considering possible consequences. Impulsiveness can create severe consequences, from school failure to life-threatening situations. Thinking about consequences before you act can help you avoid many crises.

Timothy was always on his cell phone texting and responding to texts from friends, even when he was driving. One day he was reading a text as he was entering the freeway, and he got into an accident. Fortunately, no one was hurt, but his parents took away his driving privileges, and he lost the freedom to come and go without a ride.

Joseph was deeply in love with his girlfriend, Emily. He kept asking her to have sex with him, and she resisted for many months. Then one night, after drinking at a party they had sex for the first time together and did not use any protection. After that, neither of them talked to anyone about what kinds of protection they might use, and they continued to have unprotected sex. Several months later, Emily told him she was pregnant. At eighteen, Joseph and Emily decided to get married and raise the baby together. Joseph realized that this path was not the one he would have chosen for himself, but with their parents' support, he thought it was the right choice, given the circumstances.

for you to do

Put a check mark next to any risky behaviors you experiment with. If you are uncomfortable writing down the answers for this activity, you can think about them instead.

☐ Smoking pot or using other drugs

☐ Drinking alcohol

☐ Drinking and driving

☐ Speeding or driving recklessly in other ways

☐ Driving while texting or talking on the phone

☐ Having unprotected sex

☐ Shoplifting

☐ Breaking the law

☐ Being promiscuous

☐ Smoking cigarettes

☐ Vandalizing property

Describe any other risky behavior you experiment with.

_____

_____

Of the behaviors you have experimented with, decide which is the most risky. When did you first start that behavior?

_____

How did you feel about yourself after you started?

_____

Were you worried about yourself when you started?

_____

Were other people worried about you when you started?

_____

What were you or other people worried would happen?

_____

Why were you or other people so worried?

_____

If you haven't talked to anybody about the behavior, whom could you tell?

_____

Where can you get support for stopping this risky behavior?

_____

_____

_____

... and more to do

What role does peer pressure play in your involvement in risky behaviors?

_____

_____

_____

Describe a recent example of peer pressure that involved risky behavior.

_____

_____

_____

What did you say to yourself that resulted in your giving in to peer pressure?

_____

_____

_____

Responding differently to the same question can help you uncover more ways to challenge the self-talk that increases your risky behaviors. Answer the question "Is it true?" five times, coming up with a new response each time. For example, if you tell yourself you would be rejected if you don't follow your peers, you could answer:

It's not true. If I don't drink, they would be happy for me to be the driver.

It's not true. I would actually be the one doing the rejecting because I want friends who don't need me to be a follower.

It's not true. They might appreciate my ability to think for myself.

It's not true. They probably won't even notice; not everyone is paying attention to what I do or don't do.

It's not true. They might think I was different, but they would still be my friends.

Reflecting on what you usually say to yourself when you give in to peer pressure, ask yourself:

Is it true? If not, why is it not true? _____

_____

Is it true? If not, why is it not true? _____

_____

Is it true? If not, why is it not true? _____

_____

Is it true? If not, why is it not true? _____

_____

Is it true? If not, why is it not true? _____

_____

---

for you to know

Students with ADHD can ask for and use classroom accommodations designed to increase their success. Sometimes teens are embarrassed about these accommodations or afraid that others will find out about them. It can help to remember that accommodations are not signs of weakness, but rather simply environmental supports that meet your individual learning needs and allow your true intelligence and gifts to be seen and developed.

Ryan was interested in many of his classes and often had original ideas about the material being taught, but his poor attention to detail led to a constant stream of negative feedback. When his papers came back with low grades because of misspelling, he began to hate school. He told his parents that he was discouraged by so many deductions for that type of error, and his parents set up a meeting with his teachers and school counselor. Following the meeting, Ryan was allowed an accommodation to minimize deductions because of spelling errors. The feedback he then received acknowledged his insight and creative thinking.

Luis was embarrassed to have special treatment in class and was afraid other kids would make fun of him if they knew. However, he found that taking untimed tests allowed him to show how much he really knew and to get grades that accurately reflected the time and effort he put into studying and learning the material.

Matthew had a hard time sitting still in class. Even when he was interested in the topic, he felt so restless that it was hard to concentrate. It was also hard for him to take notes because handwriting was so difficult for him. His teacher allowed him to quietly leave the classroom for a brief break, and he would return without disrupting the class. He also had a note taker so he could have all the material covered in class to study for his tests.

for you to do

Describe your feelings about using accommodations in the classroom.

_____

_____

_____

Put a check mark next to any statements you can say to yourself to feel better about accommodations.

- ☐ "I have a learning difference, not a disorder."

- ☐ "Small changes can allow teachers to see my natural gifts."

- ☐ "One size never fits all, and I need adjustments to learn best and fulfill my potential."

- ☐ "Accommodations allow me to get the grades that reflect what I've learned rather than reflecting my test-taking ability."

- ☐ "Every person has different learning needs, and accommodations are one way of meeting my needs."

- ☐ "Accommodations will allow me to perform better, which will open more doors of opportunity for me."

- ☐ "When teachers get to see what I really know, they will be more likely to see my true potential and encourage me to fulfill it."

- ☐ "Accommodations are the support I need to develop the skills I need to learn."

Write any other positive statements you can think of to encourage yourself to learn more about and use the accommodations that are available to you.

_____

_____

_____

_____

_____

_____

_____

... and more to do

Some people learn best with hands-on experience and have a hard time when the classroom teaching style is lecture only. Some are creative writers or original thinkers who are not given credit for their skills because their test scores are based only on correct answers.

Describe as fully as possible how you learn differently from others.

_____

_____

_____

_____

Describe your natural gifts that are not given credit in the school system.

_____

_____

_____

_____

What changes would help you use your natural gifts to get good grades in school?

_____

_____

_____

_____

_____

Take steps to see if any of the supports you need are available as accommodations. Typical accommodations include:

- Special use of computers

- Note takers

- Untimed tests

- Permission to make up missed work

- Alternate assignments

- Alternate grading, such as minimizing deductions for minor errors

- Homework help

- Special seating assignments

As you learn more about yourself and the accommodations that are available, you can ask your parents to arrange a meeting with someone from the special education office at your school to determine what is possible.

35 what makes a good friend?

for you to know

Most teens are more affected by their friends than by their parents. It has even been said that looking at your three best friends can let you know where you are heading. When you think that what your future looks like may depend on what your friends are like, you may want to reflect on your friendships. Much of the drama in high school is caused by people happy to find someone to hang out with, without "qualifying" friends by asking themselves if these people can be trusted to be caring, honest, reliable, and supportive.

Adam easily became friends with just about anybody. He was very open and honest, and he often told new friends about his ADHD and the medication he took to manage it. Some of these friends didn't fully understand what ADHD meant but knew only that Adam took psychiatric medications. They began to tell others that there was something wrong with him and he had to see a psychiatrist. Some kids thought this meant they should be wary of Adam, wondering what was wrong with him and backing away from him.

Andrew wrote a letter to a girl he was interested in, telling her about his feelings for her. He later found out that she read the letter to other kids and laughed about it. His feelings were deeply hurt.

Rebecca's friend Alyssa partied a lot and often smoked pot. Rebecca stayed close to Alyssa because she was more socially connected than Rebecca. After several weekends of watching Alyssa make a fool of herself, Rebecca wondered why she was friends with her. When she tried to distance herself, Alyssa began to say negative things about Rebecca to others.

All these stories share one thing in common: these teens fell into friendships without "qualifying" their friends.

for you to do

Write the names of three of your close friends, and write a paragraph describing each.

1. _____

_____

_____

2. _____

_____

_____

3. _____

_____

_____

Read through all three paragraphs and write five words that describe the qualities these friends have in common.

1. _____

2. _____

3. _____

4. _____

5. _____

Now write a paragraph describing the future you imagine for each of these friends.

1. _____

_____

_____

2. _____

_____

_____

3. _____

_____

_____

Write a description of the future you imagine for yourself.

_____

_____

_____

Present behavior predicts future behavior; you should consider the likelihood that someone who is not trustworthy now will not be trustworthy in the future. With that idea in mind, do your closest friends "qualify" as friends? Will your friendships be fruitful, inspiring you to become more of what you are capable of becoming? Or will one or more of these friendships create problems down the road? Do you want your future to look like the future they seem headed toward? Describe your reflections.

_____

_____

_____

_____

... and more to do

If you have discovered that one or more of your closest friends do not "qualify" as friends, you can begin to create a plan for finding others who do. Rather than focusing on cutting off ties with those friends who don't "qualify," you can simply decide what kinds of friends you do want and actively seek ones who share your values and interests and goals.

Write down the names of three people you would seek out as friends because you see them as caring, honest, reliable, and supportive.

1. _____

2. _____

3. _____

What actions could you take to initiate a friendship with one or more of these people?

_____

_____

_____

What activities or clubs could you join to find people who likely share your values and whom you could easily respect?

_____

_____

_____

36 how to succeed in love

for you to know
Some romantic involvements will lead to disappointment, and others will lead to caring, fulfilling relationships. Looking carefully at the personality of the one you are interested in or involved with can help you make wise choices in your love life.

Brandon's girlfriend was everything he had ever dreamed of—or so he thought. She was beautiful and fun to be with. But after they had been together for a few months, he began to notice how demanding she was. She always wanted to go on dates to the most expensive places and expected him to be available around the clock. She cared about the kind of car he drove and was very critical if his clothes weren't stylish enough. He was worried about staying with someone who was so high maintenance, but he reminded himself that she was easy to talk to and was always the life of the party.

Francine was dating the guy of her dreams. When she first met him, she fell in love with his good looks and intelligence. But as she spent more time with him, she began to get annoyed that he argued about everything, always playing the devil's advocate. Although she knew he had a heart of gold and was totally devoted to her, she began to wonder if his tendency toward debate was too much to deal with.

Jessica was in love with her boyfriend, who was attractive and charming. He was also intelligent and kept her thinking and inspired. But she couldn't trust that he was faithful to her, and she wasn't even sure she could trust everything he said. Sometimes she wondered if he had a hidden agenda for their relationship.

for you to do

Brandon, Francine, and Jessica each had to make a decision that was highly personal. In making similar decisions in your own life, you will need a lot of information to judge whether a relationship is likely to be successful. One way to gather this information is to think of the person you are interested in or involved with as having these three layers.

The Superficial Side (Brandon's story)

This surface layer refers to a partner's personality traits and level of attractiveness. A person can be shy or outgoing, fun or serious, assertive or passive: traits that become obvious within a few dates. Many people also make decisions about whether to date someone on appearance alone. Others use a partner's popularity in school as the main factor in deciding whether to begin or continue a relationship.

Describe the superficial side of the person you are interested in or involved with.

_____

_____

_____

_____

The Daily Dose (Francine's story)

Some people are irritating, stressed out, easy to be with, woefully disorganized, or super orderly. Over time, a person who is more controlling might be harder to have a relationship with than one who is more easygoing. How a partner's personality affects you can change as a relationship continues.

What would a daily dose of this person be like?

_____

_____

_____

_____

The Core Essence (Jessica's story)

At some point, you will gain a sense of the core essence of a person. Is this person solid gold? Easy to trust? Predatory? A born wanderer? A person's basic nature reflects whether a relationship will be likely to last. If you want a long-term relationship with someone, a central quality to look for is trustworthiness.

Describe the core essence of this person.

_____

_____

_____

_____

… and more to do

If you are wondering whether a relationship will succeed or lead to disappointment, try peeling away the layers of the superficial side, the daily dose, and the core essence. The most important factor should always be whether you are passionate about your partner's core essence. Daily problems can be resolved with improved communication skills and other relatively easy fixes, but it is foolish to believe that you will be able to make changes in a person's basic nature. It might be tempting to be with someone whose attractiveness and charm impresses your friends, but if you are looking for a relationship for the long haul, focus on the core essence.

Review your descriptions of the person you are involved with or interested in. Then tell whether you think this is or could be a healthy relationship or not, and explain why.

_____

_____

_____

_____

_____

37 spending time in nature

for you to know

Spending time in nature can help you focus and concentrate better. When you are building muscles, you need time to rest between sets; similarly, time in nature allows your mind to wander and roam without being constantly vigilant. In fact, recent research shows that time in nature has measurable and specific benefits for those with ADHD, including improved concentration, increased ability to follow directions, and decreased disruptive behavior.

In history class, it often seemed like Aaron was not paying attention. He would stare out the window, looking at a faraway mountain and wondering about the animal and plant life there. He wished he could learn more about ecosystems.

After class one day, his teacher gently asked him what he was looking at outside the window. Aaron told her, adding that he felt like he needed time outside to "recharge his batteries." Rather than hearing his comments as unrealistic, his teacher told him that in some countries time in nature was recognized as a basic need. She said, "In Finland, most kids learn in their classrooms for forty-five minutes. After each study period, they get fifteen minutes for physical activity outdoors. And Finland is ranked number one in literacy and among the top five countries in math and science!"

Although his teacher couldn't give him the time to go outside, she understood that Aaron's gazing out the window was his way of taking care of himself.

for you to do

There are many different activities you can do in a natural setting. Circle three activities you will commit to trying this week; use the blank lines to add your own ideas.

Walking in a park

Hiking

Biking on a nature trail

Walking in the rain

Sleeping outdoors

Bird watching

Fishing

Lying on the ground and watching clouds

Lying on the ground and looking at the stars

Climbing a mountain or hill

Swimming outdoors

_____

_____

_____

After you have tried these activities, describe any change you notice in your ability to focus and concentrate.

activity 37 ✳ spending time in nature

... and more to do

For one week, write down how many hours you spend in each of these categories.

	School and Homework	Creative and Artistic Activities	Computer Activities, TV, and Movies	Shopping	Nature	Other Recreation
Sunday						
Monday						
Tuesday						
Wednesday						
Thursday						
Friday						
Saturday						
Total						

Write down your reactions to the way you spend your time.

_____

_____

_____

Notice how much time you spend in nature compared to other activities. If you are not spending much time in nature, what areas are you spending a lot of time in?

_____

_____

How could you spend more time in nature and still get other activities done? For example, could you do your homework on a picnic table outside? Could you write in your journal in a natural setting or do your creative work outside?

_____

_____

_____

Ask your parents how much time they spent in nature when they were growing up. Compare their experiences with your own.

_____

_____

_____

38 reaching for the stars

for you to know

Many teens with ADHD struggle with underachievement; they know they could do better but somehow don't. Looking at whether your current behaviors are in conflict with the goals you have for yourself can help you increase your motivation to achieve more.

As a young boy, Joshua loved to play with Legos. He could work on kits designed for much older kids, and adults would often wonder how he could create such complex buildings. It was no surprise that he wanted be a mechanical engineer, someday building real cities.

As he got older and school felt more and more difficult, Joshua began to lose motivation and his grades slid. His dream of going to a good university and getting a degree in engineering seemed far off. But instead of facing the conflict between his lack of effort in school and his long-held dreams, Joshua avoided his feelings by watching TV shows on his computer. Every time he felt anxious about falling further behind in achieving his goals, he had a quick and easy distraction.

His parents were concerned and arranged for him to see a coach to help him with his schoolwork. His coach first asked Joshua to tell him the story of where he was in his life now. Joshua told him that he often argued with his parents about grades and that he was discouraged at how much time he spent hiding out in his room, pretending to do homework. Next, the coach asked him to create an ending to the story that showed Joshua achieving his goals.

Over time, by focusing on what he actually had to do to achieve his goals, Joshua was able to turn his grades around and gain confidence that he could go on to be an engineer. As he realized he could change his behavior to reclaim his dream, he began working harder and became even more motivated.

for you to do

There can be many different causes of underachievement. Put a check mark next to any that are relevant for you.

☐ Stress

☐ Lack of family support

☐ Too much family pressure

☐ Distraction by video games and TV

☐ Lack of interest in school

☐ Preferring to spend time with friends

☐ Being too disorganized to create a schedule for schoolwork

☐ Anger at parents

☐ A belief that school is not important, that it doesn't relate to the real world

☐ Giving priority to other interests, such as sports or playing in a band

Describe any other causes of your underachievement.

_____

_____

_____

Write a story describing your current situation. You might want to include the causes of your underachievement and your feelings and reactions to it. You might also describe how you avoid any conflict between your current behavior and your long-term plans for yourself, for example, by turning to drugs or alcohol, playing video games, listening to music, or like Joshua, watching TV.

_____

_____

_____

_____

_____

_____

Write a new, happy ending for your story.

_____

_____

_____

_____

... and more to do

Answer the following questions to increase your motivation for facing your underachievement head-on.

How can an underachiever become an achiever?

_____

_____

_____

How can someone with a handicap succeed?

_____

_____

_____

Do you know someone who successfully broke a bad habit? Ask how that person changed and write the story here.

_____

_____

_____

Write down four short statements telling your parents and teachers what you want them to understand about you. Try sharing them with your parents and teachers.

1. _____

2. _____

3. _____

4. _____

39 identifying your support systems

for you to know

It's much harder to solve your problems or achieve your goals without support. The more people and resources you can identify to help you, the more easily you will achieve your social and academic goals. You can also begin to build support systems that will grow over time.

Evan knew he was in big trouble in his math class. He had always just scraped by in math, and this semester's class was known to be the hardest. When he told his older sister that he was really worried about how he could get through, she suggested starting a regular study group.

That sounded like a good idea, so Evan asked three other kids in his class to start a homework group that would meet for three hours once a week. They encouraged each other and helped with specific problems and solutions, and they all agreed that getting through such difficult material seemed easier when they did it together.

At one meeting, the kids in the group brainstormed a list of other resources they could use to get help. Their list included their math teacher, the library, a free online homework help resource, older brothers and sisters, parents, parents' friends who were good at math, other students who were good at math or had taken this class before, the resource teacher, the disability office for accommodations, and the school counselor for help with time management.

Evan's innovative idea helped him keep motivated. His attitude stayed positive through the rest of the semester, and he passed the class easily.

for you to do

Circle any resources you already use, but can use more often.

School-related resources

Classroom teachers

Resource teachers

Other students

Librarians

School counselors

Mentors

Tutors

Study groups

Personal resources

Friends

Siblings

Parents

Other relatives

Parents' friends

Neighbors

Therapists and counselors

Coaches

Support groups

Create a list of resources that you have heard about but haven't used.

_____

_____

_____

_____

... and more to do

For each category below, write the name of someone you can ask for help and then a specific problem that person would be most useful for.

Friend

_____

Parent

_____

Sibling

_____

Other relative

_____

Parents' friend

_____

Neighbor

_____

Coach

_____

asking for help 40

for you to know

Once you have identified resources, you need to take one more step—asking for help. Asking for help can make the difference between surviving and thriving. The better you become at asking, the more resources and support you will find flowing into your life. The main obstacle to asking for help is the fear of getting rejected. If you can practice collecting rejections, you will overcome your fear of hearing no and realize that you can't be hurt by asking for help but you have much to gain.

Jordan needed a summer job to provide spending money and to help him to start saving for college. He went to several movie theaters and put in applications but was not getting any job offers. At a meeting with his guidance counselor, she said, "Jordan, it's a good idea for you to work in an area where you not only earn money but also build your skills. Can you think of any areas that interest you?"

Jordan said, "I might want to sell real estate. If I worked with a real estate agent, I could learn more about sales and business." At his counselor's suggestion, Jordan asked his parents and some of their friends if they knew anyone in real estate he could talk to. He came up with three names and e-mailed each of those people to ask whether they could help him find a paid job in real estate. Through those three people, he got contact information for ten more people who might be able to help. He e-mailed all ten and found two who were willing to meet with him.

Later that week, Jordan met with those two people and asked for a paid job. One of the real estate agents offered to hire him for some basic tasks he could use help with. Jordan asked for ten dollars an hour and received it.

for you to do

You can practice asking for help in many different areas. Put a check mark next to three things you will try this week.

☐ Ask your parents to help you find a job.

☐ Ask a teacher for a different assignment, if that's on your list of accommodations.

☐ Ask a teacher for clarification of homework.

☐ Ask a friend to help you find a date.

☐ Ask another student to help you with homework.

☐ Ask a resource teacher to review the list of accommodations you are allowed.

☐ Ask for a leadership position in an organization you belong to.

☐ Ask for tenderness from your parents.

☐ Ask for a date.

☐ Ask for advice and guidance from people who have achieved something you want to achieve.

☐ Ask a higher power for comfort and guidance.

☐ Ask for honest feedback from your friends and family.

☐ Ask a friend to help you organize your room.

☐ Ask someone in your family to help you with time management.

☐ Ask a teacher to listen to you.

☐ Ask someone you want to be friends with to spend time together outside of school.

☐ Ask someone on your sports team to practice with you.

☐ Ask a friend to exercise with you.

☐ Ask to be respected.

☐ Ask someone to suggest a person who can help you solve a specific problem.

Tell what happened when you asked for the three things you checked.

_____

_____

_____

... and more to do

To think of other things you can begin asking for help with, fill in the blanks below.

I want _____

I need help with _____

I wish someone could help me _____

I need guidance on _____

I need feedback on _____

I need clarity on _____

What is the next thing you will ask for? Write it here: _____

_____

Lara Honos-Webb, Ph.D., is a licensed clinical psychologist in private practice in the San Francisco Bay Area. She is author of *The Gift of ADHD, The Gift of ADHD Activity Book, The Gift of Adult ADD,* and *Listening to Depression.* Her work has been featured in *Newsweek, the Wall Street Journal,* and newspapers across the country. She has appeared on national radio and television programs. For more information about Honos-Webb and her work, please visit www.visionarysoul.com.

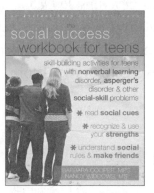